PRESENCE-BASED PARENTING:

HOW TO PARENT WITHOUT FEAR IN AN AGE OF ANXIETY

By ALI MILLIKAN

Presence-Based Parenting
Copyright © 2018 by Ali Millikan

Cover Illustration: Be the Light Photography
Author photos: KCB photography

For more information or to contact author see:
www.aliincali.com
www.experiencegodproject.com

ISBN: 9781977028310

To Sam, Anna, Eli and Joy
I love you

TABLE OF CONTENTS

INTRODUCTION

Do you ever read other people's Christmas cards or look at their social media pictures and feel a low level of fear start to rise that they have magically figured out how to raise amazing kids and you haven't? Or do you ever find yourself zoning out while your child tells you a lengthy replay of her tetherball game at recess? Or your child wants to snuggle at bedtime and you find yourself falling asleep while he is telling you stories from his day? Parenting is a nonstop job. Even vacations are just parenting in a different location.

So how do we remain present and engaged with our children rather than checking out internally or even externally? How do we increase our ability to be present in the places and with the people who matter most to us rather than be spread thin? How do we parent with confidence and without fear?

Sam was born spring quarter, my last year of law school. Added to this poor timing, he was our first child. And, as with any first child, I had no idea what I was doing.

I had one week—spring break—to figure out what to do with this child that was due any day. We didn't know if the baby was a boy or a girl. We had a few names we were batting around. I had an idea of my "birth plan" but nothing solid.

So, armed with about 10 books on everything from labor and delivery, sleep, how to change a diaper and what kind of diaper to buy, my husband and I went to a friend's cabin and spent spring break trying to wrap our heads around what was about to happen.

Then, after more than 48 of the most painful hours of my life, we had Sam.

As I held him I was overwhelmed with love, fear, the fragility of this tiny human and how little I knew about taking care of him. For the first time I appreciated hormones and instincts that filled me with a fierce love for this person whom I knew nothing about, but was mine.

Panic struck when the hospital entrusted us with a human being and told us to take him home: I could represent a client in court, give a talk to large audiences, organize a trip for college students halfway around the world, but take care of a baby?

Two weeks later, I strapped my son into a car seat, put on a suit and drove him 20 minutes to my parent's house to drop him off so I could go to court to represent a client. He screamed, I cried, but I was on a time deadline. I couldn't stop and give him what he wanted. In my mind, there went my perfect child. I had damaged him already.

I didn't necessarily know what I was doing or wanted to do, but I did know I was afraid. I was afraid of messing this child up. I was afraid of feeding him the wrong food, which would lead to health issues later in life. I was afraid of not attaching to him enough because at two weeks old I had to leave him 15-20 hours a week.

Fear can go on and on and if we don't pay attention all of a sudden fear is parenting the child. And we lose sight of the purpose in parenting: love.

But what does love look like? It is one thing to say, "I love you." It is another to back those words up.

Now over a decade into this parenting thing, I've found that love is having our heart stay open and connected to our child through the different seasons of life. Love is being present. But that is easier said than done.

The sheer physical work of parenting makes even showing-up difficult. We end up leaving our sunglasses on top of the car, dinner in the oven and forgetting to pick up a kid on time.

When my third child was 3 months old I took my children to a pool with a friend. I was so pleased with myself. I had their swimsuits, towels, sunscreen, water flotation devices, snacks, and water. I got my baby to sleep in his car seat and set him under a table in the shade to sleep by the pool so that I could keep an eye on him. I got the other two all ready for the pool and then took off my shorts and t-shirt to climb in myself. As I walked down the steps to the pool, out of habit, I made sure my swimsuit bottoms were covering my bum. But what I felt was not my swimsuit bottoms. It was 10-year-old, sheer white underwear. I had forgotten *my* swimsuit.

No one had seen me, but instead of discretely backing up and putting on my shorts, I screamed "AHH I'M IN MY UNDERWEAR."

The silenced pool patrons eyed me with horror, all except my friend, who almost went into labor she was laughing so hard!

This book is not an attempt to tell you to do more. It is a desire to help you be okay doing *less* and feel less afraid. Being present with my child just doesn't seem like enough and yet it is one of the hardest and most important parts of parenting. My child should speak Chinese, play the violin, do year-round club sports, excel at school, and be emotionally intelligent. Our brains are filled with to-do lists. Our culture values busyness. Our desires and fears drive us to say yes to more things than we have time for, making it not only hard to be physically present but mentally and emotionally engaged as well. If your family can do all that and stay connected that is awesome.

But if it can't, then how do you navigate the choices, the unknown and the fear in such a way that you have time to look your child in the eye and listen to how they are doing? Being present with our children is one of the hardest and most important pieces of parenting.

My goal in this book is to give you tools to navigate the myriad of decisions, choices and competition for your time and energy by helping you actually **prioritize your priorities**.

1

YOUR CHILD'S HAPPINESS IS NOT YOUR JOB

Sam was 4, Anna was 18 months old and Eli was a newborn. We were living in a friend's basement while we sorted out housing. To get to our car, we walked around the yard, up a grassy hill to the driveway. This wouldn't be a huge deal except it was Seattle and that means most of the time it was wet and muddy.

Greg, my husband, was already at work and I had a meeting to get to. Sam was in a stage where sock seams were his nemesis. They had to either be non-existent (who knew you could buy seamless socks) or in the exact right spot. Usually, once we survived the sock battle it was onto his shoes which were unpredictably either amazing or the worst thing ever. This particular day I was incredibly tired and late. I didn't have creative energy to get socks and shoes on. So I started with firm commands. That failing, I moved on to bribes, then ultimatums. Finally I tried scaring him into getting his socks and shoes on—I yelled at him. The socks remained on the floor and Sam continued to protest.

So with a newborn car seat in one hand and a toddler on my hip, I grabbed Sam by the hand and dragged him across the yard, up the hill to the car. Since he was now screaming, I shoved him into his car seat, shoe and sockless, and forced him to sit still while I wrestled his three point harness into position. Then with everyone in the car I proceeded to my meeting where I smiled and pretended I had everything under control.

I used to be pretty convinced that if my children did things my way they would be happy. But they didn't agree. And usually I couldn't make them. Now, their friends are no longer the children of my friends. They pick out what they will and will not wear and I have no idea what they eat at other people's houses. In fact, I've never been able to control them and that is probably for the best.

They don't want to be controlled; they want to be connected, with me. And that is what I want with them, a connection from my heart to their heart that means they understand their decisions affect me just like mine affect them. This is what I call a heart connection. To build that connection, my presence is required.

Presence requires at least two things: first, the **time** to be physically present; second, the **emotional capacity** to be engaged.

Finding time to be present cuts at one of the biggest things we talk about in our culture: how busy we are. Between jobs, strenuous schools, extra curricular activities, doctor appointments, and social events, it isn't hard to go days without eating dinner all together as a family. So in order to talk about presence we have to talk about priorities.

What *are* your priorities? What is your goal in parenting and how do you keep that main goal the center of your family life?

In all the various jobs I've held, at some point my boss either told me my goals, or we figured them out together. But, as a parent, no one has ever sat me down and asked me my goals. In fact, if I listen to the world around me, there are so many goals that I can get spun around and all I want to do is to close my eyes and take a nap. Am I supposed to create happy kids? Organic kids? Super athletes? Get them into a good college? It is so easy to feel like what I am doing is never enough. And, according to social media, everyone else's children are doing more and doing it better than mine.

The goal we intentionally or subconsciously choose in parenting dictates what our parenting looks like and how we choose to spend our time. For example, if my goal is my child's happiness, then my decisions are going to revolve around what I think will bring happiness. If it is to create independent and successful citizens, then I am going to push them to my understanding of success. Our goals are revealed by what we prioritize and what we value.

If you aren't aware of your goal then pay attention to your fears. What are you afraid of? Often our fears end up guiding our decisions whether consciously or not: fear of our child not getting the opportunities we want for them; fear of exposure to sex, drugs, alcohol; fear of their loneliness or rejection by peers. The list goes on. Without a clear purpose in parenting we become so busy trying to ease our fears that we find we don't actually have time with our kids.

Generally, you want to pick a goal that you can accomplish. I can't actually control or accomplish the goal of my child's happiness— only they can, which means if I make *their* happiness *my* goal, then to accomplish that goal I have to control them. Of course it is a desire of mine that they are happy, but that isn't my goal. A goal in any job should be something that I can eventually check off of a list. I have a goal that I finish this book by a certain date. As a lawyer, I have a goal to meet with each of my clients in person before meeting them in court. You get the point.

It is not my job, or goal to make my children be all that they can be, it is theirs. It may be my desire for them to be all they can be, but only they can do that. It *is* my job to be present to them as they navigate the myriad of decisions before them.

As a parent I have a goal to stay connected to my children. With our relationship as a safe practice place, I want my kids to get to know who they are and how to operate healthily in this world. I can only control my half of the connection. My children can choose to lie, stay guarded from me, and they can even choose to hurt me. I cannot control that. What I can control is what I do with my time and my heart.

I have different tools which I think help accomplish my goal both in connection to my children and empowering them to be engaged with the world around them: teaching them emotional intelligence, giving them opportunities to learn about who they are and how the world works, giving them opportunities to fail and practice resilience. All of these are things I can do, but **I cannot control what they do with them**. I have a desire that my children have friends, are happy, succeed at something, fail at something, learn to control themselves. But none of these things are in my control.

So, if I can differentiate between my goal as a parent (things in my control) and my desires for my children (things I may not be able to control) then it is easier to make decisions that help accomplish my goal.

Presence, relationship, heart connection all take time. Frequently I find that our desires for our children to get good grades, be top athletes, play musical instruments, have friends, and have once in a life-time experiences, all end up actually getting in the way of what may be the main thing: our connection with them. The desires aren't wrong, it is just getting our priorities straight in our mind in such a way that fear doesn't end up controlling our schedule and our relationship with our children.

At 7:20 my son meets with the other neighborhood boys to ride to middle school. One Monday morning it was 7:15 and I still had not seen any sign of him. My first instinct was to run up to his room, wake him up, and rush him out of the door. But my goal is heart connection. Waking him up and projecting my stress on him would not be helpful towards that goal. Nor does it help him for me to take away his responsibility.

I actually want my children to mess up so that they can learn while it is safe to do so. Sleeping through your alarm as an 11-year-old is better than when you have a job or even are in high school. But to help me stay out of it I have to remind myself: **this is his problem not mine**. If I make it about me, then it becomes a whole different problem. I'm not late. He is. And we have established that his waking up, making his lunch and getting out of the door is his responsibility not mine. He showed up in a panic at 7:40. Because this wasn't my problem I could authentically be present to him. We didn't problem solve why he wasn't awake on time until later. By 7:50 he was on his bike to school. And it turns out I was right—sixth grade is a great time to forget to set your alarm. The front desk staff and teachers were kind and I'm pretty sure he won't forget to set his alarm anytime soon.

A key part to empowering my children is to not take too much responsibility for how they feel. This doesn't mean I don't have empathy for and with them. But I don't make their emotions my responsibility. When you have an infant and they cry, usually it means they need something and it is your job as a parent to give it. We get good at guessing, trying different things to help the baby calm down. Then the baby is 2, and throwing a fit because they want that eye-level candy at the grocery checkout stand. Now if I take the same approach to them as a baby, my goal would be to help them feel better—buy the candy. But one of the crazy things about parenting is that your job is constantly changing. Loving a 2-year-old is different than loving an infant. If I don't adapt with my toddler, pretty soon he or she will figure out that to get what they want, they just need to throw a fit.

Last week my 4-year-old asked me, "Mom, why do you give us so many choices?" I laughed. She is my first child to consciously realize one of my key parenting strategies: choices. I give them choices all the time. My children give me choices and each other choices. It is part of how I've learned to help them make their own decisions and help them learn self-control. So when the toddler is throwing a fit about wanting candy, I give him a choice.

My kids always get to choose one thing at the grocery store to share with the rest of the family. Generally I tell them that they can have the candy bar if they put back their other choice object and are willing to share it. If that doesn't work then they can choose to spend their own money. If they have no money, they can put it on their wish list. The emotion of "needing candy now" isn't mine to fix, but it is my job to help my child know what to do with those desires.

Getting into a habit of taking responsibility for a child's feelings of sadness, stress, or anger can be dangerous. We can create children who think it is other people's job to make them feel better. It doesn't teach self-control or empowerment. It is my job to teach them about their emotions, how to name what they are feeling and figure out healthy responses to move through what they are feeling. It is their job to use those skills. I want my children, as adults, to be able to figure out what they are feeling, why they are feeling that way, and what to do about it. I don't assume they automatically know now. It is one of my jobs as a parent to teach emotional intelligence, which requires presence. It takes time listening and understanding what my child is going through to be able to coach them through how they are feeling, how the other person is feeling, and what to do with those feelings.

If I am afraid of what people think, stressed, exhausted, or overwhelmed, it is much easier to just give a kid the candy bar. But if I know my child, know my goals, then I can navigate it without fear. It doesn't mean it is always fun though!

That moment in the grocery store when your 2-year-old is throwing a fit isn't the moment to teach your child about sugar or about what they are feeling. That comes later. And please hear me, sometimes you buy the candy bar and other times you just let your kid scream it out while you pack your groceries, pay, and leave.

I have heard it said that all parenting choices fall into one of three categories: my decision, my child's decision or a shared decision.[i] One of the challenges of parenting is that what goes in each of these buckets is constantly changing. When my son was in preschool it was my decision what time we got to school. By middle school that decision has been moved to his bucket.

One of the reasons I may be tempted to take too much responsibility for my child's feelings or for their situation in life is because I want my children to know I care about them and their desires.

Creating a connection between my heart and their heart takes time. It is so much easier to step in when they are facing a problem and fix it for them. This is what we did when they were babies to care for them, pick them up when they fell down, feed them when they were hungry. But as they get older, more and more things get transferred out of my bucket and into theirs. Showing I love them becomes more dynamic than caring for their needs as they learn to care more and more for themselves.

Your child's happiness in life is not your job. It is theirs. Loving them is your job. Sometimes we approach loving our child as taking responsibility for their happiness. And sometimes this actually works against what we really want which is connection. What does being present look like for you and your family? What is your goal as a parent?

APPLICATION

Take a few minutes to reflect on what is your ultimate goal as a parent. Write down anything that comes to mind. Don't judge yourself. Look at both what you want your goals to be and what they really are based on how you spend your time, energy and money. What desires do you have for your children that are different than goals? You can go back later and decide whether or not these goals and desires are worth keeping or not. If you don't know, here are some other questions to help you figure out.

1. Why do you parent?
2. What do you want for your child or for you as a parent?
3. What is your goal in parenting?
4. What are your desires in parenting?
5. What are you afraid of?
6. Where/when/how do you take too much responsibility for your child's emotions?

7. How would you define your job as a parent, your agenda?

8. What are some decisions that belong in your child's decision-making bucket that are still in yours?

2

YOUR HAPPINESS IS NOT YOUR CHILD'S JOB

I was in Trader Joe's with my three children, three months pregnant with my fourth. My husband was gone for a month for work and we had recently moved to a new state where I knew no one. We had just had the worst stomach flu I have ever experienced. I was exhausted and overwhelmed. All I wanted was to get some things we could eat and try to make it a little fun for my kids.

So, dragging my three kids age 5 and under, I decided they could pick out stuff they wanted to eat. I said yes. Rather than just one choice they got multiple. I said yes as long as it wasn't going to make us hurl. As we were about to get into the check-out line a woman approached me to tell me that I shouldn't spoil my children so much and that I needed to do a better job feeding them. Outwardly I nodded, exhausted and slightly shocked. Inwardly I thought, "You have no idea, lady, what this is about. How dare you judge me?"

This woman voiced out loud what a lot of us as parents live in fear of—other people's judgment or opinion that as parents we are messing up. We are afraid of what others think. We know, whether right or wrong, other people may be watching and judging us. Not only that, our culture lets us know that our children should always be under our control and that any sign they aren't under control is a negative reflection of our ability as a parent.

These beliefs are lies. They end up working against what we really want, which is connection with others and with our children. The truth is I cannot control my kids – any control I have is an illusion. They are *choosing* to do what I want out of fear of punishment, desire for reward, or because they want to. The other truth is, that my identity, value and significance as a human being are not dependent on my child. Knowing these truths is one thing. Actually living them is another matter.

I started parenting thinking it was my job to control my child. Then, when my eldest was 3 years old, I read a book by Danny Silk called "Loving our Kids on Purpose."[ii] Silk goes to lengths to show that we cannot actually control anyone but ourselves and for some of us we can barely do that. Many of us try to control our child's behavior through fear of punishment, rewards and sometimes even anger. The terrible two's and teenage years are hard in part because we find our children difficult to control.

Anyone with a newborn knows you can't control a baby. One of my most embarrassing moments happened three months into parenting. My firstborn was a few months old and we were visiting a friend's church. In this church the childcare center gives you a number and if your child needs you they flash your number up on the screen. Sure enough 15 minutes into the service my child's number flashed up front. Off I went to see what was going on.

"We think your baby is hungry," they said. I knew that he wasn't hungry because I had fed him 20 minutes earlier. He was probably tired.

Before I could say anything they ushered me into their "breast-feeding room" which looked like it used to be the broom closet but now had a love seat squished sideways into it. Five minutes after I sat down, another mom came into the room with a very small baby. They closed the curtain to the closet we were sitting in to give us privacy. I'm not kidding you. Our bums touched as we tried to feed our babies on the love seat. Awkwardly we didn't even make eye contact but gave a small nod and then continued feeding our babies. It was then that things started going downhill.

A volunteer from the Sunday school came in to chat with my sofa partner. There was no room in the "room" so she stood in the doorframe. "We actually didn't page you for your baby, we wanted to talk to you about your 6-year-old. We have tried everything we can, but he will not cooperate or listen to us. He is really disruptive and aggressive towards other kids in the class and so we are going to have to kick him out of Sunday school."

Mom: "How long has this been going on?"

Sunday school teacher: "For the last three months."

Mom, trying to talk through the tears: "My husband, his dad, was sent to Iraq three months ago and my son has been really struggling with it."

Sunday school teacher: "I am so sorry to hear that but there is nothing we can do at this point."

Meanwhile, I am completely stuck. To get out of the room I would have to literally sit on the other mom's lap and ask the Sunday school teacher to move out of the way. I felt so awkward and uncomfortable and tried my best to remain as invisible as possible. I was completely lost in both my sadness for this mom and my discomfort when the mom exclaimed, "There is water leaking on my face." I looked down and my son had stopped nursing. I was now spraying the woman in the face with breast milk. This woman's husband is fighting in Iraq, her son is getting kicked out of *Sunday school*, while she's breastfeeding a newborn, and now, some stranger's bodily fluids are spraying her in the face! I have never wanted to become invisible so badly.

I wish I could say I handled it gracefully but I covered myself back up, grabbed my baby and got out of there as fast as I could. I was so uncomfortable and embarrassed that I couldn't be present with this other mom or with my child. I was worried about what *they* thought of *me*.

Parenting is a humbling job. As much as I like to pretend I know what I am doing I frequently don't. It is easy to make decisions out of fear of what others think of me. But then my perceived sense of their opinions ends up parenting, not me. The last 12 years of parenting have been a process of learning how I parent, who my kids are, which voices to listen to and which to drown out.

I often confuse presence with power and confuse power with love. Being present with my child doesn't mean I am using my power to control them. Being present is being emotionally and relationally engaged with my child. When I have a heart connection, I don't need to solve their problems or use my power to take care of them in order to show that I love them.

For example, frequently when we are all sitting at the dinner table my 4-year-old wants something: a different color plate, or milk instead of water. So, we ask her to get it herself. Just as frequently, she then throws a mini-fit wanting someone to do it for her. If there is any part of me wondering if she knows I care about her, then I'm tempted to do it for her. But because I'm convinced that we have a heart connection and this isn't about love, I actually think it is disempowering to do it for her. This is a task she can do on her own.

We are too afraid to let our children experience pain or to experience the consequences of their actions and so we feel the need to use our power to step in and remove the consequences. This is in part because we believe our kids represent us and in part because we honestly don't want them to get hurt.

But it is also because we have redefined love. Love becomes equated with caring for their needs, and removing pain. If I really loved my child I would drop off their lunchbox that they forgot. But in the process we are making things worse for them: we are just delaying the consequences of our child's actions to when they are older and we aren't around to protect them.

I'm not suggesting that we shouldn't protect our children. But instead of always doing the work for them, we can be teaching and showing them life skills in order to empower them and help them learn to protect themselves.

As a parent, I make sure they know how to cross the street, to not talk to strangers, or not to touch something that is hot. I teach them how to do their homework, tie their shoes, use money wisely, be kind, and fix messes they make with friends. I teach them how to ask for forgiveness, make their bed and have manners when they eat. What I am doing is empowering my kids to be able to enter the real world and thrive. I want them to be the best version of themselves.

But at some point I can't enforce my sense of what is right. While they are little we can grab their hand and prevent them from running across a busy street. But we can't control our teenagers as they cross the street. I can show them how to organize themselves and get their homework done but I can't do it for them. And if I do, then again I am crossing the line and using my power to control rather than to be present. Our children need to have self-control, learn from their decisions and they need to know how to choose wisely.

So, what is the line between disempowering our children and stepping in to protect them? We create these little mini humans. We have all the power. In the beginning we do everything for them. As a parent, my job is to gradually give more and more power to my children so that by the time they arrive at adulthood they can be individuals who can control and take care of themselves.

I vividly remember holding my first born as a 1-week-old and realizing how powerless he was. As he has grown older we have shared more and more of the power with him. He gets to choose. He gets to go through the consequences of his actions and learn from his mistakes. That doesn't mean we withdraw from him, but we don't rescue him either. As he moves toward his teenage years he wants more and more freedom and autonomy. He knows, because it is a constant conversation that with more freedom comes more responsibility, that he can choose to stay up as late as he wants if he can handle the consequences of being tired.

One of the ways we have tried to empower our children is through information and an open dialogue about cultural norms. Our goal has been to be the ones teaching our kids about life, letting them know the cultural norms and being able to dialogue about it.

Take sex. We want to be the experts in our kids' minds. So as soon as they started asking about how the baby got inside my body, we would tell them. For the 2-year-old, the story was that a part of dad goes inside a part of mom and releases sperm that combines with an egg, making a baby inside mom's uterus. But before our children started elementary school we wanted them to know the basics about sex with proper terms. When they are little, kids don't know to be embarrassed by it—it is just fact. The other night at dinner we had a whole conversation about all the slang terms for scrotum and penis. I want my children to know and then to understand the appropriate uses. My first grade boy thought this was so funny he could barely eat. But then all of the terms they heard on the playground came up. "Oh that is what the boys are talking about when they talk about that..."

Being able to have open conversations helps me stay connected to what is going on with my child. Giving my children information empowers them.

But in order to empower my kids, to give them some of the control, I have to let them fail, make mistakes, and be disappointed. And in order to be okay letting my children fail, I have to separate my identity from theirs.

How much of your happiness is dependent on your child's happiness or success? If our identity, our enjoyment of life becomes too closely attached to our children, then we don't give them room to fail and learn from their mistakes. In order to be present with someone, we have to give them space to be themselves.

Your happiness cannot be your child's responsibility. It is your responsibility. It is easy to say that, but honestly, as parents, we become too enmeshed in our child's world and their success and failures end up becoming ours. Whether or not our second grader wins her soccer game becomes a big deal, because we want her to be happy, because we want to be happy. But seriously, how much does that game really matter?

When we attach our identity to our children, when we make it their job to make us feel good, then the natural response is to attempt to control them. We want to control what people think about our child because ultimately that is a reflection of us.

Let's take a very real scenario where my child is turning in sloppy, bent, torn homework and wearing clothes that have holes in them. There are two ways I can approach this situation.

If I am afraid of what people think (their teachers or other parents) my natural response is to try to control. "You can't wear that." "Fix your homework." Depending on my philosophy I might even withhold something to motivate them to change—no screen time until you can start taking care of your homework.

If I am not afraid of what people think then I can help my child understand what is culturally appropriate. "When you turn in your work the teachers and future bosses aren't just looking to see if it is completed but how well you've taken care of it. Part of how people will treat you in our culture is dependent on how you present yourself. Wearing dirty disheveled clothes to your school communicates a lack of care." Then, once I have taught them the cultural norms, figured out with them why their clothes are dirty and homework is torn, it is up to them to act. I can help them learn what is the norm, help them create systems for their homework to keep it from getting ruined, but, without fear, I don't need to control them. They can choose.

In order to help me not control my children and their homework situations, I frequently have a conversation with new teachers. I'm a bit type A when it comes to homework. I was never late in turning something in. But my kids are not me. So I like to let the teacher know that we are engaged with our children, but we have taken the approach to support them when they need it but not do their work for them. I really don't want to be the nagging mom. So as long as we create a space for them to do work, help them understand time management, I let them do their homework. Every teacher I have talked to has been in complete agreement. So, when they have late homework, or fail a spelling test, I am clear with myself, my child and the teacher that this is the child's problem, not mine.

How much does your identity or significance depend on how well your child does? How much do you try to control them and what others think?

What are you afraid of? If you look at your children, or think about having a child, what are your fears? What are you afraid of happening if your child fails at something? What are the fears beneath those fears?

If we can acknowledge and name our fears, then they start to have less power over us. We can then recognize when we are responding and motivated out of fear. Fear frequently leads to trying to control, in order to prevent what I fear from happening. If I am afraid my child will be late, I am going to control the situation—including my child—in order to not let my fear happen. If we can pay attention to our fears, then rather than letting the fear take over as the parent, we can practice self-control and empower our child to learn.

It makes sense if I am emotionally connected to my child, that when they are sad I would be sad, or when they are struggling with something it would affect me. I'm not saying that we shouldn't have empathy for our children. What I am saying is that our identity has to be separate. While their failures or struggles may affect me emotionally, they shouldn't call into question my own sense of success or failure. Their loss at a soccer game does not mean my failure as a person. Similarly, their success doesn't mean my success as a person. I can celebrate with them, but I have to remember that my significance is independent of their performance. My happiness is not their job.

APPLICATION

Again, take a few minutes to think and write about the following questions:

1. How much of your happiness as a parent is dependent on your child's successes and failures?
2. Are there ways you are using your power as an adult to control your child, instead of empowering them to make their own decisions?
3. How can you empower your kids more?
4. What are you afraid of happening to your kids?
5. In what ways are you letting fear dictate your parenting?

3

KNOW YOUR CHILD

I have two boys and two girls. It is amazing how kids from the same family, with the same parenting approaches can develop so differently and have such opposing personalities.

One child at 2 ½ years old asked us about the difference between Santa and God and if they were both real. Another child at 2 ½ couldn't speak in complete sentences. One child wants to be home as much as possible, while another is always asking where we are going next. A heart connection takes on a different shape with each one because they are different people. The way they bond, communicate and relate is unique.

There are three tools I have used to get to know my kids. The first is prayer. The second is time away by myself. The third is various personality inventories.

I believe that God knows our children and that God gave them to us. This means that as we figure out who our children are, we have help from someone who knows them better than we do.[iii] I believe that God is good, that God is for us as humans, that God speaks and that I can hear in part what God is saying. I'm not always right. It has taken me years of practicing on my own and with other people to learn to tune in to what God might be saying as opposed to other voices like my own voice, fear or the culture around me.

While each of our children was either a baby or still in utero we prayed over them with a group of friends, asking God "who have you create them to be?" We then wrote down what we heard in prayer. This is called listening or prophetic prayer. For each child we came away with different words, phrases or images about their personality.

Friends had multiple pictures and words of one of our daughters singing, loving music and being a song. When she first started eating solid food, around 6 months old, she would hum as she ate. I didn't teach her that, no one else in the family does that. As a toddler she loved to sing. Now, not only does she love to listen to music, she frequently gets songs in her head, either new ones or ones she knows, that speak to her and encourage her. This is the way she senses God speaking to her. A song will pop into her head that addresses something she is feeling, like anxiety or fear and the words to the song comfort her.

With each child we wrote down up to 10 things that either we or other people had received in prayer. I put the list in the front of a journal I have for each child. I refer to the list at times to remind myself who they were created to be, not to confine them to that, but to encourage.

They also have a copy of it and during times when they feel discouraged, insecure, lonely or afraid I like to pull out the descriptions and words to remind them that God knows them and they are a good creation. It also helps them remember the ways they are unique and special.

For one of our children the descriptive pictures had a theme. They all involved conquering mountains and overcoming obstacles. Sure enough when he started to crawl rather than go around obstacles he went over them. As he has gotten older, not only does he try to find ways over obstacles, he creates obstacles to get over. His energy and impact is nonstop. There are days where it simply overwhelms me and the pictures from before he was born help me partner with him rather than shut him down. They help me be patient and channel his energy and creativity because I believe this is part of who he is created to be, something to be trained not squashed.

The second way I've spent time figuring out who my children are, is through an annual retreat. Years ago, I was in a small group with a woman whose children were older than mine. She taught me the value of an annual prayer retreat focused specifically on my kids. Before having children she had been in business. Every year, they would take a couple of days away to figure out their goals, strategies, what was working and what wasn't working. She started doing the same thing for her children.

She would dedicate a day per child (she had two, so with four children I take half-a-day per child) and leave for one or two nights. It was her annual business retreat where she refocused her goals, desires, and plan as a mom for her children. She structured it into three different parts. First, for each child, she would start by writing out everything that he or she was doing well and anything she was thankful for. Second, she would transition to three areas of growth for her child. Finally, my friend would write each growth area down and spend time asking God for Bible verses to pray over her child until the next time she could take some time away. For little kids she tried to get away quarterly since they change so fast and are so exhausting! For older children she moved to once a year.

When we moved to Scotland, one of my four was having a hard time. She was struggling with confidence and anxiety. I went away for about four hours—and used an hour per child to pray and process through what that child needed. As I was praying for her, the idea of horses popped in my head. Horses are not apart of my background nor are they something I had ever considered for my daughter. I really had no idea where to start. As I got to know people in the community, we found a woman who taught children how to ride horses at a very reasonable rate. We started our daughter with lessons. Being around horses and learning to ride really helped her confidence personally. After she started school, we figured out that three of her closest friends also had lessons at the same barn. Horses became a central part in her connecting with friends.

Now three years later, we have moved again. This transition has again been hard for our daughter. Where we are now, riding is more expensive. A friend informed me about a ranch not far from our house in Oregon that gives free lessons a couple times a month and pairs each child with a mentor, who not only teaches the child to ride but also spends time getting to know and encouraging the child.

Our daughter came home glowing from her first session. As she explained to her instructor, horses are a huge help for her to move through her emotions. She feels like she can express how she is feeling to the horse and they won't make fun of her or judge her. She feels free to be herself, comforted, and encouraged. We had our last session of the season a few weeks ago and my daughter sat and chatted with the same instructor she had started with. It was such a gift to know there was a trustworthy adult listening to my child, as well as teaching her to care for and ride horses.

Horseback riding wasn't on my radar. It came through time away praying for my child and listening to any insights God might have for her. Then, even after hearing about it in prayer, I was pretty convinced it was out of our budget, but God provided a way.

Lately, my prayer retreats have been more like prayer mornings. I take four hours at a coffee shop, one hour on each child. I use a separate notebook for each kid. That way I can look back on what has happened since the last time I wrote and prayed.

I begin with a letter to each kid, describing what has been going on, what they like, dislike, what they are up to, friends, struggles, and triumphs. Then I start a written conversation with God, thanking God for everything I can think about for that child.

Finally, I ask God to highlight two or three areas for each child that need some attention. Over the years this has been as simple as learning table manners, to as big as anger-management. Then I ask for wisdom and discernment as to what will help that child in that area. When they finish high school, I plan on giving these journals to them. That way they can see the different ways God answered my prayers.

The structure of the retreat doesn't matter as much as the concept of taking time to go away and refocus. Spending time thinking about the bigger picture, away from all the to-do's and daily needs, helps me keep track of what is going well and what needs some attention. It helps me with our decision-making—like finding a place and time for my daughter to be around horses. It also helps me be present to our children because it fine-tunes where to put my time and energy.

There is no way as a parent I can meet the needs of each child. Their needs and desires seem infinite. As they grow older, they need to figure out what they need and desire and what it looks like to advocate for themselves. Prayer has been central in helping me understand my role in their life at each particular season.

It has also been significant for my children to learn to pray about things outside of their control. All three of my older children have had experiences praying for what seemed like the impossible and watching it happen. The answers have rarely been immediate and usually that child has gone through some pain in the process, but in the end they have concrete ways they have experienced God caring for them and their desires.

The third tool I use to get to know my children is personality tests. My kids have never taken a personality test. But, through books and trainings, my husband and I have familiarized ourselves with a couple of different tools that have allowed us to watch the patterns in our kids' behaviors and desires and start to get a picture of their particular personality and preferences.

First we looked at love languages. My kids really enjoy a picture book that explains different love languages.[iv] This is the only "personality test" that our children actually self diagnosed. Love languages include quality time, quantity time, physical affection, gifts, service and words of affirmation. For one, quantity time (spending a large chunk of time together doing a shared activity as opposed to quality time which can be an hour over coffee with good conversation) is important. For another, it's physical touch. Giving lots of gifts to my child who feels loved by spending time together ends up a waste. He would rather the cold hard cash or for us to rent a movie, get some ice cream, and put the other children to bed early so he can have time alone with us. It is fun having my children self diagnose their love languages and try to take care of each other. For my daughter's birthday, all of her siblings work extra hard to give her presents because they know they mean a lot to her. If our ultimate goal is to be present with our child it helps to know how to communicate presence and love and it helps a little go a long way!

Second we looked at what motivates our children. I didn't really think about this until I got married and was faced with this reality that my husband is not motivated by the same things I am. Tradition means very little to him. Just because we went ice skating last Christmas

Eve doesn't necessarily mean we should this Christmas Eve. Money, people, tradition, history, fame, changing the world or appearances are all different motivations for people.[v] Appealing to tradition in order to motivate someone who is primarily motivated by money just won't work.

The motivators test[vi] splits people's primary motivations into six categories. For most of us we have a couple different primary motivators depending on our circumstances and a couple that don't really motivate us at all.

First, a *socially* motivated person has a love for helping people and will make decisions based on what is going to be best for others. They are motivated to drive two hours to make a baby shower or stay up late to pick someone up from the airport.

Second, *aesthetically* driven people care about external beauty and/or internal harmony. Whether arts, fashion, interior design, a high value for nature and beauty, or relational harmony in work and home life, this person is motivated to adjust their surroundings to fit what brings them peace. This person may find the lighting and the way their office looks to give them headaches or make them anxious. Or it could be that working in an environment with a lot of unresolved conflict wears on them physically and emotionally quicker than someone else.

Third, an *individualistic* motivation is a drive for power. This person has a desire to make an impact in the world and may be competitive and assertive. They will work the extra hours and do what is deemed necessary to rise to the top, be noticed and network in order to improve their work and social standings.

Fourth, *theoretical* people have a high value for the pursuit of truth. This is a more cognitive motivation and this person may value knowledge and education for education sake. This person is motivated to take the time to get to the bottom of things, to make sure the facts are correct or to become an expert in something.

Fifth, a motivation for *tradition* is motivation to follow the rules, the way it has been, for both order and unity. They may find a break in the way it always has been to be stressful and confusing. "We always get the Christmas tree, on this day, from this place and put it here."

Finally, there is the *utilitarian* motivation. This is a motivation for money and what is going to be most useful. For this person driving two hours for a baby shower may not be the best use of time and money. They may figure out a more cost effective place to get the Christmas tree this year.

There are a lot of different personality inventories, from the Enneagram, Myers Briggs to the DISC behavior test. Obviously children are still developing, and so all of this has to be held loosely. We used the DISC to understand our children a little better. It discusses innate behaviors and how people are going to respond in various circumstances. Here are some brief summaries, which we have found useful.

The D in the disc stands for *dominance.* Some of the words used to describe this personality type are "decisive, brave, problem solvers, visionaries, pioneering, results oriented, ambitious, big picture thinkers, delegators, directors, assertive, bold, adventuresome, innovative, change agents, confident, courageous, competitive, and take us places we normally would not go."[vii] Certain people are wired to behave in a dominant way—I like to think of it as a bulldozer.

All children have a bit of a bulldozer in them as they sort out their desires and boundaries. But we have one child who is a bulldozer about everything both physically and with his desires. Not only does he like to find obstacles to get over, he is tenacious about practicing until he can make the jump, score the goal, catch the ball, skate backwards, and on and on it goes. He would rather do something alone than be flexible and play with someone else. He will push to get things done a certain way. Understanding the "D" personality type has helped us train him rather than squash him. For example, teaching him to be "fun and flexible" and figure out healthy responses to not getting things his way.

The "I" stands for *influencer*. This person is the life of the party. They come up with lots of ideas and love to be the center of attention. They can move quickly and be spontaneous, often acting without thinking things through first. Act first, fix later. They see the glass half full and are positive, encouragers and collaborators. One of our children shows influencing behavior. She consistently enjoys situations more than others, and can work a room at a party. It is always amazing to me to watch my different children experience the same events but react so differently to them.

Steadfast or "S" people are team players. They like to serve others and you can depend on them to come through. They may prefer to be in the background, setting things up than running the show from up front. They work slower than an influencer or someone who is dominant but like an influencer they are people-oriented instead of task-oriented. Again, one of our children shows steadfast behavior. She needs more time to work through things, loves to help and serve. She likes to know the plan and have a routine. She doesn't necessarily want the lime-light but wants to be around people.

Finally there are "C's" who are *conscientious*. Like someone who is steadfast, they enjoy a slower pace but similar to the dominant person, they are more task-oriented. They are the planner, researcher and rule-follower. This means they like to research the best product for the best price even if it takes more time. Someone with a "D" or "I" behavior type might prefer to save the time and spend the money. A "C" values excellence and will take extra time to make sure they are speaking the truth. Again, one of our kids is very conscientious. He likes to research everything to make sure he is making the best decision, and hates having things sprung on him. He likes smaller groups of people and working independently.

Of course in all of these there is our natural style but we adapt and change based on circumstances. You may find yourself a misfit in a culture or family system dominated by other behavior styles. For example if your work environment consists primarily of *"D's"* or *dominant* personalities and *"I's"* or *influencers* who like to act first, and plan later, move fast and think of truth as something that is "in the ball-park" but you are a *"C"* or *conscientious*. You may experience considerable stress at having to make decisions so quickly, move at a faster pace and have coworkers who define truth differently. Similarly, having a child who is an *"I"* or *influencer* and loves to be the center of attention, in a family that is primarily *"S"* or *steadfast* and values serving behind the scenes, may lead to conflict and tension.

Again these tests aren't to pigeon-hole my children but to help me appreciate their differences. So, when I have a child who needs more time to understand and figure something out, instead of getting impatient with them, I can appreciate this is part of the way they are wired and work with them from there. It also helps navigate conflict between my project-oriented kids and my people-oriented kids. Both need to learn to be sensitive to the other and to understand. It helps me figure out which child is wired to need more space and help them figure out ways to get it. It assists me in helping them navigate other people and the way their brains are wired.

Despite all these tools, each child is still a mystery and changes as they grow up. Without putting our children in a box, prayer and other tools have helped us discover how to maintain a heart connection with each child in the midst of their uniqueness. Presence looks different with each child.

APPLICATION

You may not have a community that can pray over your child, nor have the flexibility or resources to leave for a weekend on your own. Regardless, take a look at your calendar and mark off some time on your own, whether it is getting up early one morning or taking an hour on the weekend. Set aside sometime somewhere. If you have more than one child, maybe just start with one. Bring a pen and paper. Start by writing out everything you can think of that you are thankful for that child. Write a letter to them about the stage they are in. Then, highlight a couple of areas that need attention. If you want, take some time to listen to God and see if God gives you any creative ideas. Here are some possible questions to ask God. Write down everything that comes in your mind in response and edit later.

1. Who have you made this child to be?
2. What are their strengths?

3. What do I do with this situation that is weighing on me?

Sometimes ideas might pop in your head like horses, piano lessons etc. Don't immediately dismiss them. Write them down. Then later ask for more help, guidance. What does this look like? Where do I go? Sometimes I think God will give you specifics and sometimes it requires us starting down the path of figuring it out and God will show us as we go.

4

KNOW YOURSELF

There are two components to being present—the **external** physical reality of creating time to be with our children but also the **internal** presence of mind to focus on the person in front of you.

Presence is not to be confused with being physically present all the time. Some of us can't spend every day or even every weekend with our children. We have jobs, we share our children with another parent, and our kids have school or other activities. This is why our internal presence is so important. Presence has more to do with the quality of time. When you are with your child do you have space internally to focus on them?

Being able to be present with someone else requires me to be present with myself. I have to be okay with who I am and I need to process my stuff in order to be able to listen to their stuff.

One of my daughter's lives in chronic pain. We have spent countless hours with doctors, naturopaths, counselors and specialists to try to help reduce some of her pain. Some days she handles it better than others. And some days I handle it better than others. She frequently wants to "snuggle" and needs extra time holding my hand or sitting in my lap. Ideally, of course I will hold her in her pain. But I can tell when I am overwhelmed and haven't dealt with my own emotions or stress when she asks for a hug and it overwhelms me.

Understanding my tendencies and preferences helps me relate to my children. So just like I used love languages, motivators, DISC inventories to better understand my children, I have also used them to understand myself.

For example, I am an external processor. I've had to learn to either find people to process with, take time to write, or go for a run because for some reason when I am moving my body it helps me process what is going on. I never have "extra time to do these things" so I've learned to get up early before anyone else is awake to write or run. It is worth the pain to get up early because it makes such a big difference in my ability to be present with my children. When I am not taking time to do any of these things, I have less patience and energy, causing stress in my children's lives. I have a harder time being present with them in their pain.

Knowing my main motivators and behavior tendencies also helps me let my children be different than me. I am not a researcher. I like to move quickly and am motivated by people. Knowing that my son's cost/benefit ratio is different than mine helps me not project my process onto him when he is making decisions.

He needs more time to think something through whereas I like to try something and then change later. While I am motivated by once in a lifetime experiences, he isn't. He thinks about the time and cost involved and may prefer to use his resources on something else. Understanding all of this helps me come alongside him instead of just pressuring him to do things the way I would.

Not only does it help to understand how I operate it also helps me to know what my issues are. As I've already said, I tend towards taking too much responsibility for my children. So when my sixth grade son gets his school schedule and he doesn't have many classes with his friends, my tendency is to call the school, show up in the administrator's office and try to work it so that he is with his friends. I can easily become that nightmare helicopter parent hovering around to make sure my children are taken care of. Instead, if I actually live according to my values, I can use my son's sixth grade schedule to help him build some resilience and teach him how to talk to the counselor if he thinks he needs a different schedule. Knowing my "issues" not only helps me navigate them but it also ensures I'm not trying to use my children to feel better about myself.

Sometimes we carry things around with us that make it hard to be present because being present requires us to face pain and the pain feels like it might break us. Pain can be from the past, from our own parents or from some situation we are currently in. It may seem easier to avoid, suppress or distract ourselves. It definitely makes it hard to be around anyone who asks anything of us, especially our children. If I am carrying around a lot of pain, then I don't have room to carry anyone else's. I am a big fan of counseling. Often the pain we have experienced in life requires professional help to move through it.

One of our kids began to see a counselor in order to process through some moving-related anxiety. The counselor's main focus was to teach our child to be present. He taught mindfulness techniques that train the brain to be present in the moment instead of escaping or shutting down.

Whenever our child started to feel anxiety, the counselor wanted him to take note of everything he could smell, hear, feel and see in the room in order to stay present to the situation. He taught presence as an antidote to anxiety, which is a useful technique as a parent.

As you attempt to be present with yourself, your partner, your children and your friends, my biggest encouragement is to give yourself grace. Our job is to love our kids and to be able to look them in the eye, listen, and give a little of ourselves to them. We will make mistakes. They will make mistakes. In the midst of it though, figure out what it looks like in your family with your different children to be able to stay present. There are good days and bad days, but it is worth it to fight for time and space both externally and internally to be able to be with our children.

Knowing where I end and my child begins helps me not take responsibility for their happiness nor give them responsibility for my happiness. As a parent we sacrifice time, energy, money, our sleep, our bodies in order to care for these human beings. We literally pour out our lives so that they can live. And in that process it is so easy for us to become empty. Understanding myself, what fills me up, what energizes me, what my limits are helps me not only care for myself but actually care for my children. I run because running energizes me. I'm actually a better parent if I take time to run.

If you are carrying too much stuff in order to be emotionally available to your children, then I would suggest talking to someone. Sometimes we can talk to a friend and other times it requires talking to someone trained to help people move through pain. Sometimes talking to God and moving through forgiving others and ourselves can help take away some of the pain. Forgiveness does not mean that whatever wrong you suffered was okay. Nor does it mean you stay or enter back into harmful or hurtful situations. What it does mean is that you are letting go of being that person's judge. Sometimes we also have to forgive ourselves for our own mistakes.

It is one thing to get to know my child. It is another thing to be aware of myself. Taking some time to differentiate between my preferences and theirs helps me keep my identity separate from theirs. When I can keep them separate, then it is easier to not make them responsible for my happiness or take responsibility for theirs.

APPLICATION

Take some time and work through the following questions:

1. A little bit about you:
- Who were you created to be?
- What are your strengths and weaknesses?
- Do you embrace conflict or avoid it?
- What drains you or energizes you?
- Where do you go and what do you do to get filled?
- What motivates you? Do any of the DISC behavior styles resonate with you?

2. A little bit about your capacity to be present:
- Are you emotionally available? If not is there anything weighing on you and what is it?
- Are you physically available? If not, is there anything you can cut out to be more present?

5

PRIORITIZE

It is one thing to know who you are and what you need, it is another thing to prioritize your needs. Yes, there are seasons in life when we have to endure pain and sacrifice and prioritizing our needs really isn't even an option. We have jobs we have to go to, bills we have to pay, and may not have time or money to get a babysitter, go for a run or get the sleep our bodies desperately need. However, there are times when a little goes a long way and we can creatively figure out ways to live according to our priorities.

Two weeks after giving birth to our first child, a woman from our church volunteered to babysit. She was amazing, trustworthy and had children of her own. Still my first thought was "I'm not letting someone else, not a part of my family, take care of my baby!" Greg, my husband, however thought differently and arranged to have this woman look after Sam while we went out for dinner. Greg felt very strongly that we needed to have a night a week where we could go on a date, even if it only lasted one hour because we were both exhausted. He was working as a youth pastor, I was finishing law school, we had a newborn and he wanted to make sure we still had time for each other. Reluctantly I agreed to go on the first date. Our son lived and Greg was right, it was really good to have even an hour of uninterrupted time to connect. So, for the first five years of parenting, people from our church volunteered to watch first one, then two, and finally three children while we went out on our weekly date.

This was one of the most important decisions we made during that phase of life. It wasn't that we always had amazing conversations or went out for a long time but we chose, and still choose to make our marriage a priority. Now, we have four kids and no longer have free babysitting so we don't have weekly date nights out of the house. But we still regularly find time just the two of us, sometimes while the kids watch a show on the weekend, or a lunch date during the week.

Someday when all our kids are out of the house, it will be just us again. My husband was right to make time together a priority so that we could continue to connect beyond and outside of all the parenting, career, financial and scheduling decisions we make together on a daily basis. Not only is it important to make our marriage a priority for our sake—it also positively impacts our children.

John Medina is a developmental molecular biologist and has written books on how the brain works. He says in his book, *Brain Rules for Babies*, that one of the biggest ways we can help our kids succeed in life is to have a healthy marriage.[viii] Even for single parents, having a stable home environment enables our children to thrive not just at home, but outside of the house as well.

It is easy to respond to the tyranny of the urgent. There is always more to do. Without a sense of our priorities we can become consumed and reactionary, responding to what seems the most pressing demand of the moment. Whether that is a child's immediate need, a work call, a post on social media, we react.

Instead, with clear priorities, I can choose what I am doing with my time, energy or even my mind. It's true we don't always have a choice, sometimes we have to respond and it is appropriate to do so. I'm talking about those areas in life we can choose. But in order to choose well it helps me to understand my priorities.

Spending time with God, my family, friends, and even myself, are all priorities. Running and writing are a priority for me because when I run and when I write I am actually able to be *more* present with the people around me. It has taken me a long time to realize that one of the ways I process what is going on inside of me is to run, and then to write it all out. When I am doing both of those regularly, I carry less around with me. When I carry less around with me, I am able to hold and carry more from those around me. I have room to engage their stress, anxiety, and conflicts from school. I can be more present with them.

Knowing my priorities means I have a clearer sense of when to say yes and when to say no. When my husband was a pastor, I was a new lawyer and we had young kids, I was asked semi-regularly to do more—either at the church or in the public defenders office. My first response was "sure"! Then, as time went on, I realized my kids and husband (the people I said mattered most to me) ended up getting the scraps of what was left. I had to start thinking through my time choices differently. I could no longer burn the candle on both ends and have it only really affect me. There are so many people who will ask of our time and energy. Sometimes, it is easier in the short term to say, "Yes" but that often means the people we care about the most get the least of us. I have had to learn to choose (when I can) to put my time and energy where it matters most.

Once we have children it feels like every relationship undergoes some change, mainly because time changes. The bread and butter of parenting is self-sacrifice. Birth mothers literally give up their body to someone else. We give up sleep, space, money, and time in order to put kids first, to provide, and take care of them.

Too often in the process of sacrificing ourselves for our children, we forget who we are. We have to be someone in order to be able to have a heart connection with our kids. We have to have likes, dislikes, triumphs, failures, and things we can share with our children so that as we get to know them, they can get to know us. We have to have places we get filled up, so we have something to give to our children.

I'll never forget the dinner conversation with our kids when it first dawned on them that we had a life before they existed. They had question after question: "What sports did you play?" "Where have you traveled?" "Have you always known Daddy?" Then they started asking for stories and in the stories they found connections to themselves. "I like to run and want to try track and field, like you ran track and field." Just as it is important for our children to learn about our past, they also need to know who we are in the present.

For example, one of my kids was really into Star Wars—he knew every detail of each universe and random species. For a long time, I feigned interest as he talked. I didn't actually care and honestly I wasn't really listening—I checked out after a certain amount of time. Unintentionally, I was training my child to think that he could talk non-stop and ignore social clues. I wasn't teaching him about how to relate to me. After a while, I had to be honest with him, for his sake. I'm actually lying when I pretend to listen but don't. I'm fake-engaging. I do want to hear an overview, I'm interested because he is, but I don't care about all the details. In fact, I can't even follow the details of the different worlds and species. So I slowly started asking him to give me an overview. I tried to help him understand how to communicate his interest to me. I wanted him to know I was interested because of him, not because of Star Wars.

Just as parenting is a process of getting to know our children, it is also a process of our children getting to know us, and how their choices affect us. For little kids, it can be as simple as learning the impact of lying. "When you lie, I can't trust you, and trust is one of the key parts of heart connection. You need to trust my word and I need to trust your word." As kids get older, it is important that they understand our desires, even our preferences, both when we exert them and when we are willing to give up what we want for someone else.

Our children learn from our actions as much as our words. We model what conflict resolution, boundaries, friendship, health and nutrition all look like. In any healthy relationship there is some give and take. But when our children are little, there is going to be almost 100 percent give, on our part. Because of that, we need to make sure we value ourselves enough to get filled back up. If you had any other relationship that was 100 percent one-sided, you would have to take breaks, find ways to be encouraged and energized. It is okay to take breaks from our children. And as they get older it is okay to let them know what we are doing and why we are making certain decisions. Not only is this modeling healthy lives, it also means we actually have something to give to our kids.

APPLICATION

Take five minutes somewhere on your own. Write down all the people, events and other things you are committed to on a daily, weekly, and monthly basis.

1. Who or what are your priorities?
2. How can your time reflect your priorities?
3. What relationships are important to you and how can you protect them?
4. How can you find time for yourself?

6

PRESENCE INSTEAD OF PERFECTION

Why do we go "back-to-school shopping" and post pictures of our children on the first day of school? Why do we think that a child should start preschool at 3-years-old? Why do kids get phones when they go to middle school? Neither wrong nor right, these are culturally assumed norms. Sometimes we may have well thought-out reasons for why we parent the way we do. Other times, it may be because that is the way our parents did it. Or because everyone else is doing it that way and we haven't stopped to ask if it this cultural norm is worth sacrificing time, energy and money for.

Often we parent without knowing why we are parenting that way. As a result we end up living stretched and thin, exhausted and stressed. Sometimes what we really want, which is for our children to know they are loved and for us to have a relationship with them that endures, gets put on the wayside while we run them from school to horse-riding and then to soccer practice.

Parenting is an important enough job that it is worth taking the time to figure out why you do what you do and what it is you actually want to be doing with your child. It is worth the time to figure out your goals, desires, and strategies just like you would at any other job.

Ironically, unlike other jobs, we won't know if we have done a good job until our really influential days are over. It is as if we are novice construction managers building a house. We've watched someone else build a house (our parents). We see other people building houses around us. And we read books about building houses. But we've never built one ourselves. On top of it the houses people are building around us look amazing on the outside. So we live in constant fear that this thing is going to collapse or blow up in our face. Are we making the right decisions? Is our kid doing enough? Have we spent enough time as a family?

Rather than building a house, I like to think we are tending a garden. In the beginning we have to do a lot of work to prepare the ground, clear the soil, remove the weeds, and plant seeds. But we can learn as we go, figure out which plants work in this specific soil, which weeds like to grow, and how to deal with them. Then as our kids get older we teach them how to tend their own gardens until someday they can do it themselves. Mistakes are okay. Learning is part of the process. Our goal isn't a perfect garden but a healthy one. Being present is more important than being perfect. Showing up is better than having it all together.

Frequently my youngest will grab my face and pull it so I am looking at her and say, "I just want to be with you." My presence helps calm her fears. It doesn't matter to her whether I've finished the dishes, am wearing the trendiest jeans, or even if I have contributed meaningfully to society. She doesn't need me to be perfect nor does she think she needs to have it all together for me to show up. She just knows she wants me there.

Presence is more powerful than perfection. If we are trying to make perfect kids, fear of inadequacy might be rational. But perfection isn't our goal. We aren't and don't need to be perfect parents. We don't need perfect children to be happy. So let's stop pretending that we are perfect and instead take time and space to be available and honest with others and with ourselves.

One day one of my kids came downstairs with a water bottle full of "juice". This child had a friend over and they both tried to persuade another child of mine to drink out of the bottle. I knew we didn't have juice in the house. After a short interrogation as to the source of the juice, I found out that my child had peed in the toilet then had scooped up the toilet-water-pee mixture into the water bottle. They had both decided to try it to see what it tasted like!

My first thought was, "How am I going to explain this to your mother?" "Hello, yes, I am sorry to tell you that under my watch your kid drank my child's urine. I *was* watching them, the doors were all open, and I had just gone to the kitchen to get a snack ready. I am so sorry!" The mother was amazingly gracious, had a good laugh with me about it and actually let her child come over to play again. The next time I decided to use their curiosity to experiment with different baking ingredients to see what happened when we put them together and put them in the oven.

Our job as a parent is to use our power to serve and empower, to be present regardless of perfection, and to love. It is to take these human beings that are entrusted to us for a season and empower them to be all they can be, to be present with them as they learn how to navigate life, and to communicate our love in the midst of both our own and their successes and failures.

My hope is for joy on the journey. Too often I try to arrive, to finish the to-do list, to get somewhere, and then once there I think I will be able to enjoy life and take time with the people I love. After 40 years of life I don't think I have ever "arrived." There is always more, better, and different. Presence over perfection requires me to stop even when everything isn't done, to look my children in the eye, and listen.

APPLICATION

Take some time either on your own or as a family to talk about the following:

1. How do you as a family handle people's mistakes?
2. Are there any culturally assumed norms in your house that you would change?
3. How do you feel letting your children, your partner or other parents see you fail?
4. Do you approach parenting more like building a house or like growing a garden or some other analogy all together?

CONCLUSION

I want my children to know in the core of their being that they are valuable and powerful. I want them to grow up understanding that they can use that power to build up or to destroy themselves, others, and the world around them. This is why presence is one of the biggest gifts I can give my children: because it communicates significance and value. They are worth my time and my attention. Being present and using my power to empower them rather than control them gives my children the opportunity to practice their power and learn how to use it well.

To recap the previous chapters, presence requires at least two things: *time* to be physically present and the *emotional capacity* to be engaged. Presence is both *physical*—I am with you and *internal*—I have the emotional capacity to pay attention to you and what is going on in your life. To be present with someone requires me to be able to be present with myself.

So, how do you determine what to do with your time? Start by figuring out your goals in parenting. Understand who your children are as individuals. Understanding your goals, your children, and yourself helps you figure out where to put your energy and focus—where to put your presence. And remember their happiness is their job, just like your happiness is your job.

How do you maintain the emotional capacity to engage? Know yourself and know your child. Prioritize. Don't let fear take control, ever.

Knowing your goals as a parent will help you as you navigate the innumerable decisions out there, prioritizing what and who is important to you.

Paying attention to your fears can help you acknowledge them but not listen to them.

And if you can truly live out that *your child's happiness* is not your job and that they aren't responsible for *your happiness*, then you have a chance at being able to be present with your child, and to stay emotionally engaged.

This is how God loves us. God is present with us even though we aren't perfect. This is love. And ultimately we all long for people who will be with us even though we aren't finished products. We want connection, to be known and to know others.

Remember—you are not alone and no one is perfect! Lets choose presence over perfection. Showing up, looking your child in the eye, listening and engaging, even for a short time, goes a long way. You've got this!

ABOUT THE AUTHOR

Ali grew up in Seattle, Washington, Scotland and France as the eldest daughter of Presbyterian mission pastors and academics. Relationship with God has always been a key part of her life and over time awareness of God's voice and presence intensified. It was as an 8-year-old when Ali first heard that there were children in parts of the world who didn't have parents. Her immediate desire was to help them have a home and access to love, care and support. This desire to serve women and children has taken many forms throughout her life from global engagement to attending law school and working in child advocacy.

Ali has put significant focus on what it means for kids to experience intimacy with God and have a place of value and significance in the world. She received a Juris Doctor, from the University of Washington School of Law and a Master's of Arts in Theological Studies, from Regent College. After working with high school and college students through different churches, Ali worked as a lawyer representing youth in juvenile court and in the foster care system.

Now, Ali finds herself in Bend, Oregon with her husband and four children, Sam, Anna, Eli and Joy. She regularly blogs on two websites: www.experiencegodproject.com and www.aliincali.com. She also finds herself occasionally speaking both locally and internationally. That said the majority of her time is spent doing the daily tasks of raising four children.

THANK YOU

It takes a village to raise a child and it also apparently to publish a book. Thank you so much for all of you who have given me feedback, encouragement and have edited this with me over and over again.

Thank you to my sister Andrea for all of your work in making this more than just thoughts on a page, putting commas where they need to go, helping me with fonts and design and helping me understand myself better as a parent! I could not have done this without you!

Thank you Libby, Monica and Erika for being extra eyes reading through this and more importantly for parenting alongside me. I have learned so much from you.

Thank you Jennie Spohr for teaching me the ways of publishing and taking time to edit.

Thank you Michelle Ruetschle for sharing your publishing journey.

Thank you Linda Rowan for encouraging me to take annual retreats and enabling me to take time away.

Thank you to "Be the Light Photography" and "KCB Photography" for the pictures.

Thank you to Julie for being a conversation partner in life and in writing. Thank you to the other women whom I have met through the years and who have laughed and cried with me on this journey of parenting. You know who you are.

I am always amazed by the reality that no matter which country or state I am in, we are all asking the same question: am I doing enough? Are my kids going to be okay? My answer to all of us is YES! More than enough!

Thank you mom and dad for making sacrifices to spend more time with us.

Thank you Chuck and Colleen for letting us live in your basement and sharing your lives with us.

Most of all, thank you to Greg my husband for parenting with me and Sam, Anna, Eli and Joy for training me as a mom. I love you.

ENDNOTES

[i] This concept is from Julie Metzger, RN, MN and Co-Founder of Great Conversations.

[ii] Danny Silk, *Loving our Kids on Purpose: Making a Heart to Heart Connection* (Shippensburg, PA: Destiny Image, 2009).

[iii] For more go to www.experiencegodproject.com.

[iv] Gary D. Chapman and Rick Osborne, *A Perfect Pet for Peyton: A Five Love Languages Discovery Book* (Northfield Publishing, 2012).

[v] Wendy Crawford, *A DISC and Motivators Guide to Understanding Me ~ Understanding You* (Plymouth, Michigan: River Heights Media, 2013).

[vi] I am certified to administer and train people in DISC and Motivator assessments. For information and pricing on evaluations and consults visit www.aliincali.com.

[vii] Crawford, 62.

[viii] John Medina, *Brain rules for Baby (Updated and Expanded): How to Raise a Smart and Happy Child from zero to Five* (Seattle, Washington: Pear Press, 2014), pg. 57.

Made in the USA
San Bernardino,
CA